WHAT I SHOULD'VE TEXTED

Also by Pierre Alex Jeanty

WHAT I SHOULD'VE TEXTED

Pierre Alex Jeanty

Andrews McMeel
PUBLISHING®

TABLE OF CONTENTS

These words are everything I wanted my
    fingers to muster up the courage to write
when your name came across my phone
    screen.
Sometimes the answer came from my brain
    telling my heart what it should say
and other times it was my silence standing
    up for me.
These are the replies that you will never
    see but that will finally leave me.

FRESH WOUNDS

The darkness of the night has painted my
   windows black;
I've robbed it of every ounce of light.
I feel comfortable in the dark right now.
   It makes me feel as if the darkness isn't
   trying to swallow me, but instead, I am
   feeding it parts of me.
The pain, however, is loud. It's telling me
   about you.
Whispering about the good moments
   that sting when they are replayed in my
   memory, like eating ice with broken glass
   sprinkles.
I will be okay,
I will not be okay.
I am fine, but no, this hurts.
I will be fine.
I am not hurting; I am processing
   heartbreak.
I don't know the difference.
I don't know what is real or what isn't
   right now.

All I know is that sitting in this dark room
   is the only thing I feel is going right.
But even that is starting to give me mixed
   signals.
I let the blue light from my screen crack
   through the darkness, to give my mind
   a break by scrolling through different
   people's ideas of happiness they want
   others to believe are truly theirs.
I could be posting about how I am happy
   about us ending to make you believe that
   I am well on my way but my timeline is
   only reminding me of you.
It's giving me mixed feelings like you did
   before all of this ended.
I am missing the life we pretended to have
   on social media.
I am missing you while wanting to get
   over you.

I am loving the peace I am finding in the
  darkness while wanting a text from you
  to break through.
I want to be interrupted and I want to be
  left alone.
Look what you've done to me.

Are you okay?
Ya, I'm fine.
Please pick up the phone.
I'm busy.
Can we talk?
Please leave me alone.
I didn't mean to hurt you.
I'm not convinced.
I'm sorry for everything.
I forgive you.
. . .
What???
I really just want to have a conversation.
Not right now, okay?
Please don't leave me.
I need some space.
I want to fix this.
Not what I need right now.
How's it going?
Good n u?
Why are you being so short?
I have nothing to say.

**Do you think we can ever be
   something again?**
IDK
Please forgive me.
I can't right now.
Do you hate me now?
No.
I never wanted to hurt you.
But you did.
I didn't mean for this to happen.
It happened.
Please give me a second chance.
Do you really think you deserve it?
Can we hang out?
To do what?
Remember this . . .
Nope.
I still care.
I don't anymore.
I think about you a lot.
Please don't.
I'm still in love with you.
Get over it.

I'm begging you to take me back.
I'm over you.
WYA?
None ya.
Why are you so mean now?
Because you broke my heart.
Let's go eat.
I would rather not.
I will earn your trust again.
How're you gonna do that?
What's up?
crickets
I made a mistake.
Sure did.
Can I see you again?
crickets
Why don't you answer my texts?
I'm over you.
I wish things were different.
Oh well.
Are you seeing someone already?
Leave me alone.

I never thought we'd be here, that things
   would be like this.
Let it go.
Why are you ignoring me?
Because you hurt me, remember?
I can't live without you.
Now you see that?
I will always love you.
Why did you let me go then?
You changed the password.
Of course I did.
You said you would never leave me.
So did you.
Are you up?
crickets

Are you okay?

I am not, but I am trying to be.
My chest feels both heavy and empty.
My hands feel too small to hold these
   shattered pieces.
I feel broken, though I know I am not.
I am not okay.
I can only pretend to be.

Ya, I'm fine.

Please pick up the phone.

I cannot surrender my ears to your words
  right now.
The heartbreak is still fresh, the reality is
  settling in.
I cannot make room for your voice to make
  choosing me difficult.
A conversation with you won't lead to good
  things, the bad is too loud right now.
I will let my phone ring until it stops, until
  I stop caring.

I'm busy.

Can we talk?

I don't want to. I do want to.
I shouldn't want to.
Maybe I should let all the anger pick up
    the call
and express every bit of what it has to say.
But then again, I will look hopelessly
    heartbroken.
Can we talk?
No, I am uncertain about how to feel
    about you,
and I will not let my heart take the lead.
I am too vulnerable, and my heart has
    written enough excuses to forgive you.
I will not talk to you;
I will only talk myself through this phase
    of getting over you.

Please leave me alone.

I didn't mean to hurt you.

How do you do something that takes so
    much time and effort
and propose that you didn't mean to?
Like you stumbled into new habits that
    use my heart as a punching bag,
like your crafted hurtful words just fell out
    of your lips.
Like you choosing to end us was just you
    getting caught up in the moment
when you've devoted so much thought to
    your decision.
Perhaps, if you suddenly felt disconnected
    and ended it, I would understand,
but even that would take time and would
    make me think you were never serious.
We didn't cancel a first or second date.
You walked out after we'd been on enough
    dates to lose count.

I'm not convinced.

I'm sorry for everything.

No, you're not.
Maybe you are, but nothing at this point
  has painted this to be true.
I want to believe that you are, but you've
  made it hard to believe.
You're sorry for everything that found
  its way into the light, your darkness
  exposed.
You are sorry for everything that can no
  longer happen.
You're not sorry; you are simply
  disappointed that things didn't end on
  your terms.

I forgive you.

. . .

I know you are searching for the right
    words to say,
the right things to offer me in attempt to
    awaken the feelings I've had for you,
like a poet trying to craft the perfect
    paragraph to crack open a struggling
    heart.
Maybe it's the guilt or my absence forcing
    you to dig deep.
I am also looking for the words to show
    how much you've hurt me and why I'm
    justified in wanting to stay away even
    when I don't want to.
So many things bubbling up inside of me
    and maybe in you.
But for now, I will stall mine and I will see
    yours as an attempt to not lose me until
    proven otherwise.

What???

I really just want to have a conversation.

Now you want to converse.
You were all tongue-tied before
making our conversations feel like a chat
    between myself and loneliness.
Still don't see how we got there
when good conversations open the door for
    us to become more than strangers.
Now that you feel yourself slipping back
    into that title,
there's sudden desire to chat.
It's tempting since I am being fed what
    I'm craving,
but I will not settle, habits don't change
    that quick.
I don't want to talk.
I want my space.

Not right now, okay?

Please don't leave me.

I am not leaving you.
You've already left us.
I am only giving you the freedom you've
    wanted.
To be single, to be alone, to be free of the
    need to communicate and all the other
    things you wanted to be free from.
I'm not leaving you.
I am making sure that neither of us are
    trapped in what we don't want.

I need some space.

I want to fix this.

I believe you can,
but I don't believe you will.
I believe it's possible.
I don't believe that you truly want to or
    believe that you will commit to it.
But I do believe you are looking to wipe
    the guilt off your lips.
Despite what I believe,
this won't be fixed.

Not what I need right now.

How's it going?

Oh, you still remember that I exist.
I am doing good, I mean bad,
I mean I am trying to act unbothered by
  what has happened to us while the pieces
  of my heart slowly fall out of place.
I am bad at pretending and good at falling
  into temptation.
How is it going?
Well, the truth is, it's not going.
I don't know how to take another step
  without you,
I don't know how to live without your
  smile, without your warmth, without
  your heart being mine to love.
Honestly, it's not going well, but I will let
  either my silence or short answers do the
  misinterpreting for me.

Good n u?

Why are you being so short?

This is the longest I've seen you crave
    communication from me.
It feels like the beginning.
It feels like when we believed nothing
    would end us.
Look at us, our relationship was as long as
    these text messages.

I have nothing to say.

**Do you think we can ever be
something again?**

There's no longer a "we," unfortunately.
Second chances are for roses that are well
planted in good soil.
We need more than water.
We never had roots, we never endured
the storms, we never overcame the sun's
breath.
Instead, our grips slowly loosened up when
anything bad happened.
I've heard that people build the most trust
during times of struggle.
We built more struggles during the struggle.
We were together but we can never be
again because we never became more
than two people playing chess with that
fragile thing between our chests.
I don't think we can.

IDK

Please forgive me.

It's something I am trying to find my way
   around.
Forgiveness, such a powerful thing, yet so
   difficult to breathe life into.
I will forgive you, not now.
I am still trying to dissolve the attachment
   into residue.
I am trying to forgive myself for choosing
   you more than I am interested in
   forgiving you.
Please forgive me.
These are words I am letting echo back
   from the mirror.

I can't right now.

Do you hate me now?

I have poured far too much love into
    loving you
that I do not have enough left to hate you.
I do not hate you.
I do not want to love you either,
but I am still working my way out of that,
slithering my way out of my emotions,
making sure I don't find any green grass to
    rest in.
I do not hate you. I have love for you.
Love that is fading into memory.

No.

I never wanted to hurt you.

In this life full of choices,
if you never wanted our love story to be on
     its last page,
why did you tear up so many pages and
     burn too many of my words?
Why didn't you choose not to let
     things end?
Why couldn't you find more commitment
     in your blood
and love in your heart to keep our
     relationship well-fed?
I may have my part, but I fought and loved
     like there were two of me.
You could've done the same.

But you did.

I didn't mean for this to happen.

Unfortunately, it did.
Unfortunately, you stabbed me right in
  the heart
while promising to have my back until the
  end of eternity.
Unfortunately, this relationship fell right
  into the cycle I've survived before and
  tried my best to avoid.
All we have as a reality is the fact that it
  did happen
and that "us" happening again is something
  I am doing my best to make sure doesn't
  happen.

It happened.

Please give me a second chance.

You are begging for the very thing I want
    to hand to you effortlessly.
My heart has been ready to open at any
    sign of light.
Like a flower bud, even the heat from the
    bridge you've burned
somehow has made me more open,
but it doesn't matter.
It's not about my willingness to give you
    a second chance but what you would do
    with it.
You have yet to see why the first
    chance died,
You have yet to have time to prepare
    yourself for another chance,
You have yet to stare at your wrong to see
    how to make it right.

I am willing to give you a second chance,
   but I cannot easily hand you a heart that
   you broke with the expectation that you
   will care for it while it is being fixed.

Do you really think you deserve it?

Can we hang out?

Absolutely not.
It's not that I don't want to.
It's the fact that I don't need to.
Yes, I miss your smell, the way you made
   me feel love.
I miss the way you made all of this
   feel real.
I will take every chance I get to make
   sure I never give you the opportunity to
   believe that we can be something once
   again.
We cannot hang out, neither will I hang on.
We can only hang all of this up.

To do what?

Remember this . . .

I remember,
I remember it all.
The way you made my heart feel protected.
The way our lips met each other
   effortlessly.
I remember the way I let love in.
I also remember the nights sleep wouldn't
   visit me because of you.
I also remember the way my insecurities
   spoke your name and my poor heart saw
   nothing more in you.
I remember how it felt when I knew
   my name no longer sounded like your
   favorite words.
I remember seeing hope fading in
   your eyes.
I remember us ending before we broke up.
I remember.

Nope.

I still care.

Why didn't you care enough to stay?
To love me,
To build our friendship.
To save our relationship,
To be with me.
When you care for something, you don't let
life leave from it.
When you care for someone, you don't feed
them heartache.

I don't anymore.

I think about you a lot.

If I'm being honest, my heart can't seem to
find a way to stop caring yet.
Maybe because this is fresh,
Maybe because the adrenaline hasn't worn
off and the pain hasn't made its bold
announcement yet.
But either way I am thinking about you.
My thoughts seem to be revolving around
the idea of you being back in my arms,
Being back in my heart, being present in
my life.
I'm thinking about you as well,
But the unfortunate truth is that not every
thought will hold hands with our reality.
The reality is that you can only be
just someone I think about now, and
nothing more.

Please don't.

I'm still in love with you.

How could that be if we are apart now?
I've heard that love is the glue that keeps
   people together.
Was it not enough for us?
How could it not hold us together when
   things got sticky?
Did you love me but couldn't find your
   way to be in love with me?
Perhaps love alone couldn't get the job
   done for us because it needed more
   from us.
Or maybe we're just good at professing
   it in messages like this and that's where
   it ends.
Either way, our love wasn't enough.

Get over it.

I'm begging you to take me back.

How fulfilling for my ego to see you
    pleading for another chance,
begging to hold my heart and get another
    chance to care for it.
Here you are on your knees; swearing to
    not lose me
It may be a dream, but you've done
    nothing to make it a reality
I will sober myself up, though it feels
    impossible.
I will not let the feelings I have left for you
    stay in my system.
It's tempting, but my feet know how to run
    away from temptations.

I'm over you.

PIERRE ALEX JEANTY

WYA?

Where your presence isn't welcome.
Where you can't read my face & throw me
   more tempting promises.
Where you can't hurt me.
Where I don't have to pretend to be okay.
Where I will be okay.

None ya.

Why are you so mean now?

After all the time we've spent together, you
   still don't recognize my defense signals.
How words are my weapon of choice.
How sarcasm becomes the perfect shield to
   keep my vulnerability well-guarded
and clear everything that can soften
   my heart.
I'm forcing myself to be mean to you.
I don't want to. I just need to protect
   myself.

Because you broke my heart.

Let's go eat.

So I can inhale the foul smell of the pain in
    the air,
and taste the disappointment while the
    truth is still hard to swallow.
Why would I order a meeting with you just
    so I can see what used to be once again?
My hunger to put broken pieces back
    together finally died.
No, we can't go grab a bite. You've bitten
    my fragile heart enough.
I will not let my ears bow to the sound of
    "what was" anymore.
I've come to my senses,
I would rather not.

I would rather not.

I will earn your trust again.

The thing with second chances is that it
summons a different type of fear.
I will no longer answer to the fear of being
hurt, the fear of being wrong, the fear of
heartbreak.
It's no longer the unknown that is standing
in the way but the known.
Now it is the fear of being hurt again, the
fear of being wrong again, the fear of
getting my heart broken again.
Fears that, if I am honest, will not give you
a fair shot.
I would love to see you squeeze every drop
of those fears out of me like you squeeze
for the last drop of toothpaste.
The truth is, I do not see how you will do
more to win my heart when you've done
less when the demands were less.
Sure, go ahead and try your best not to
prove me right.

How're you gonna do that?

What's up?

Nothing is up, nothing is down, nothing is
    sideways anymore.
Nothing is close to being the way things
    were before with you.
The temperature of my emotions is still up.
The way the pain uses my heart like a
    thermostat ranging from cold to hot,
    there's too much going on in this body I
    call home.
What's up? Maybe it's the sky, but for
    now it's a ceiling of regret I am trying to
    break.

crickets

I made a mistake.

Did you?
Or did you not expect the outcome to be as
    unfavorable to you as it's been.
I want to believe that it was a mistake, but
    my brain won't let me.
Even my heart can't see the "oops" in your
    decision.

Sure did.

Can I see you again?

Why would I put myself in such a position?
My eyes have seen enough of everything
  you have to offer and every magic trick
  you've built in the name of potential.
You can see me again,
from the other side of the burned bridge,
where the scars become meaningful tattoos
  on my heart with lessons
that I will repeat to my grandkids when
  I tell them stories on how to recognize
  false love.

crickets

Why don't you answer my texts?

Because I don't need to,
even though I want to.
Because I'm trying to get over you.
Because I want to let go of even the idea
  of you.
Because I have no more words for you.

I'm over you.

I wish things were different.

I wish the same.
I wish I had met someone different.
I wish the unmet promises were different.
I wish the way I love you could've been the
    difference.
I wish you were different, or I had
    different taste in lovers.
The unfortunate reality is that my wish did
    not come true, and we had far too similar
    of an ending.

Oh well.

Are you seeing someone already?

I am indeed seeing someone.
I am getting to know the person who
   promises to never let me down again,
the person who is finally accepting all the
   love I have to give.
The person I needed to become for so long.
I am seeing me, I am caring for and
   loving me.
I don't have time to chase any more
   heartache.

Leave me alone.

I never thought we'd be here, that things
  would be like this.

I did, but I didn't want it to.
I convinced my gut that the alarm kept
  going off because I was full of it.
Full of fears from my last relationship that
  needed to be flushed.
Every suspicious feeling I had, I convinced
  myself that it was my insecurities.
Here we are, guilty of what you said you
  wouldn't do and what I've been expecting
  you to do.

Let it go.

Why are you ignoring me?

I am not ignoring you,
I am being who you were to me in the
relationship.
I am being absent when you are craving
my presence.
I have the door to my heart closed when
you are asking me to come inside.
I am acting single the same way you've
done it.
The difference is I am not acting, I am
single and better off without you.

Because you hurt me, remember?

I can't live without you.

You couldn't live with me either.
You made existing in my presence a burden
     to you.
Let all the good things I had to say fall onto
     deaf ears.
You celebrated my absence like a holiday.
How can you not live without me now,
when living with me was a reality you
     needed to escape from?

Now you see that?

I will always love you.

This right here is something I am learning
   for myself,
To always love me, to always put me first.
I am learning to believe the same words
   when I speak them to the mirror.
I will always love you, a lie you once
   told to me that I will now turn into my
   affirmation
until it becomes a reminder that love will
   always keep people like you far away
   from me.

Why did you let me go then?

You changed the password.

Yes, we do not share anything anymore.
I've had to reset my heart to help it learn
    new meanings to words it has heard
    from you.
Words that were supposed to always be
    associated with love but now seem like
    vowels for hate.
Words like "I love you."
Yes, I changed the password.
I am getting rid of every letter, your phone
    number, and every symbol that was
    attached to you.
I changed it, just as I am making these
    hard changes.

Of course I did.

You said you would never leave me.

And you said you would never hurt me,
  but here we are.
Yes, I may have spoken this once, but the
  conditions weren't unconditional.
That promise was crafted for someone
  I believed would hold my heart in their
  hands until death forces them to drop it.
You're not that someone.
You've dropped my heart quite enough
  times.
It may take me some time to gather all the
  pieces together and leave for good,
but I am still leaving because you've given
  me every reason to.

So did you.

Are you up?

Yes, finally learning to not fight sleep but
    to surrender to it.
Yes, I am up.
Watching movies that no longer create
    pools from my eyes.
Yes, I am awake, carrying good
    conversations with friends.
Yes, my eyes are wide open to the love of
    my family and to the truth of us.

I am awake and done with you.

crickets

PICKING AT SCABS

The blue light hijacked my pupils while
my mind surrendered itself to scrolling
through an endless feed of perfectly
crafted words, filtered images, and ideal
lives.
I am passing time and thinking about the
time that has passed since our book of
love became a bunch of ripped pages,
broken spine, and perfectly crafted words
all scrambled as empty promises.
You are finally gone, or I think you are.
"Out of sight, out of mind" is doing its
magic.
"No more text, disconnect from ex" is
becoming my new tune as well.
Let's see how it goes.

Heyyyy
What's up?
You were right about everything.
Oh really?
I understand now.
Good for you.
Can I come over?
No, you cannot come over, it's over.
Is it really over between us?
Yes, it sure is.
Take me back.
Why would I do that?
Sorry for the way I treated you.
I appreciate you apologizing.
I miss your face.
What do you miss about it?
Can I get my stuff back?
New phone. Who is this?
I just want my stuff back.
You reminiscing yet?
Why would I be?
You sound a little selfish nowadays.
Oh really?

Remember the fun we had with the lights off?

Get over yourself.

Are you seeing anyone?

Why do you want to know?

Are you single? Seriously.

Not really.

We had good times together.

What was your favorite?

You're always sending mixed signals.

No, I am not.

I took you for granted.

A little too late for that.

Can we at least be friends?

No, we cannot.

We can make this work.

That won't happen.

You're ignoring me?

crickets

Happy Birthday

Thank you.

How did you celebrate your birthday?

Enjoying life without you.

It's been good knowing you. I'm moving
   on. Wish you the best.

K

Why are you always responding
   with "K"?

Okay.

I don't want to lose you.

You did lose me.

I'm miserable without you.

crickets

We had good times together.

Whatever.

You look nice.

Are you stalking me?

You deleted me on Facebook?

Yes.

Are you with somebody?

How's your new friend?

Do you miss me?

NO.

I go back and read our old texts.

Good for you.

You deserve better.
I know this now.
Can you please help me?
I cannot.
Are you busy?
Stop bothering me.

Heyyyy

Here you go again.
Just when my heart is starting to catch its
    breath, here you come knocking.
I've lasted enough days without standing
    on the fact that I don't need you.
I love that you are using "y"s to make sure
    the tone isn't misinterpreted.
I am using those "y"s to ask the right
    questions.
Why now?
Why try again?
Why are you back to making this hard
    for me?
Why won't you find a way to live in the
    past after leaving me?

What's up?

You were right about everything.

How sweet it is to hear those words
   coming from you.
Like honey pouring into my ears.
And the thing about honey is that its
   maker stings.
You stung me in all the wrong places,
I've grown allergic to you.
But even now when my lips are buzzing
   to say "I told you so,"
I won't tell you so.
Seeing you finally see things I always
   hoped you'd see doesn't take the
   swelling away.

Oh really?

I understand now.

What do you understand now?
That second chances ought to be earned.
That anything you don't want to die, you
    must water it, or at least protect it.
Do you understand that I am gone, that
    I will be the one who got away, even
    though the reality is that you pushed
    me away?
I hope you understand love.
I hope you understand commitment.
I hope you grow to understand yourself.

Good for you.

Can I come over?

For what?
To pretend like yesterday was sunshine
and rainbows when it was a flood of
everything I've never expected?
Clouds of disappointment raining on my
heart, leaving dark clouds over my trust.
Why would I let you come over . . .
when all you'll do is paint better lies on top
of your lies
and make emptier promises to fill in your
previous ones?

"Can I come over?" only makes my mind
scream "can it be over?"

No, you cannot come over, it's over.

Is it really over between us?

You've always had trouble reading
   the room or reading my heart, so I
   understand.
Yes, it's over.
I have poured out every drop of water my
   body can get rid of without collapsing
   from my eyes.
I have created this invisible scale to
   properly weigh the good and the bad.
I've done a lot of soul searching.
I've thought about everything, and they all
   encourage a life without you.
I'm comfortable without you now. I see
   why I need to live without you.

Yes, it sure is.

Take me back.

I will not revisit the past.
There's nothing there for me, not even you.
I may have contemplated what
   reconnecting would look like, but I've
   found too much good in our disconnect,
   too much peace in your absence,
   too much joy in being outside of a
   relationship with you.
I cannot take you back; it will take me too
   far back.
I've been doing too much work to lose
   progress for hope in something that was
   once hopeless to me.

Why would I do that?

Sorry for the way I treated you.

Please don't apologize.
Without your mistreatment, I would not
  have known what I shouldn't accept
  from someone who let "I love you" slip
  through their teeth.
Please don't say you're sorry for being
  yourself,
for showing me the best way you know
  how to show that you're not in love
  with me.
I'm sorry for not understanding this sooner,
  for not trusting your actions sooner, for
  not closing the chapter sooner.
I'm sorry for misinterpreting your
  mistreatment; please don't be sorry.

I appreciate you apologizing.

I miss your face.

What do you miss about it?
The way you managed to keep it tear-
  stained.
The way you managed to color my eyes
  in red.
The way you whispered so many things to
  it while having a mask over yours.
What do you miss about it?
Is it the nose that couldn't smell your lies?
The cheeks that welcomed your kiss freely?

What do you miss about it?

Can I get my stuff back?
New phone. Who is this?

How convenient to switch to your next
 page already.
To cut off my character from your story
 already
when you just promised that you will fight
 for your role.
I know you might be pretending.
This is stepping more on my heart while
 it's dead.
Thank you, I guess, for reminding me why
 I am better without you in my life.
Maybe I needed to stop texting you while
 emotionally drunk.

I just want my stuff back.

You reminiscing yet?

You texting me when you are reminiscing
is only giving life to the worst memories
  I've had of you.
You know what will always be better than
  reminiscing?
Committing to a love story that reminiscing
  isn't the only way
to keep the good times alive.

Why would I be?

You sound a little selfish nowadays.

When choosing yourself is a race, you've
 committed
to coming in last every single time.
People who were in first place will always
 question it
when they have to surrender their position.
Yes, I've become selfish because rewarding
 selfish people with selflessness
hasn't been fair to me.
It's like pouring water on dead plants with
 no sunlight, no fertilizer,
nothing but blind faith and foolish hope.
To be clear, it's not selfish.
It's me putting myself first, which forces
 me to take out the things
that keep me from being myself.
You.

Oh really?

Remember the fun we had with the lights off?

I remember the dark times I ran into
　　because of you.
I remember how my insecurities started
　　speaking louder because of you.
I remember how you put me down more
　　than how you put it down.
Please, keep these conversations as far
　　away from me as possible.
It's a turnoff.
It's reminding me why I need to make sure
　　there aren't any cracks for you to sneak
　　your way back in.

Get over yourself.

Are you seeing anyone?

Are you seeing your nose in my business?
Or seeing yourself trying to bring back to
    life something you stole life out of?
Why do you care about who I'm seeing
    when you didn't care to see me when
    I was with you?

Why do you want to know?

Are you single? Seriously.

I am single.
I cannot afford to put my heart out in the
    dating pool when it's currently drowning.
I can't afford to enter another relationship
    when I'm still shutting down the door of
    the old one.
I am still insecure with trust issues. I am
    too hurt to love right now.
I am single and entertaining absolutely no
    one, but I will not let you know that.
You think my singleness is another word
    for loneliness or another green light to
    find your way in.

Not really.

We had good times together.

Here you go again, trying to cast bait to
    motivate me to admit.
To admit that I am still reading your texts.
To admit that I am only replying to see if
    there's a flicker left between us.
I am still holding on to something.
I know it's not much, sometimes I don't
    know what it is exactly, but I know I am.
Let's be clear.
The good doesn't substitute the bad times.
When good times are nothing but fading
    memories, they become worthless.
We had some great times together,
but I am ready for some even better times
    with myself or someone else.

What was your favorite?

You're always sending mixed signals.

Of course you believe that's what I'm doing.
Communicating through our phone line
   will make you believe that you have the
   perfect signal to move in, but that's
   not true.
You just have limited access to me though
   it's supposed to be no access at all.
The resistance I give you confuses you.
Sadly, it's no magic trick, no strategy,
   nothing deeper.
Just uncertainty trying to find its right
   shoe so it can start making an exit out of
   my life.
Remember how confused it left me in our
   relationship?
Now you see what it feels like to be on
   the other side when someone is unsure
   whether they want to be with you or not.
Pretty soon, I'll be able to send you no
   signals at all.

No, I am not.

I took you for granted.

Yes, you did.
Seems that we are both coming to the same
   conclusion.
The realization may be giving you reason
   to come back,
but it's giving me every reason to keep you
   away from my path.

A little too late for that.

Can we at least be friends?

Absolutely not.
I do not trust myself around you,
and I do not trust you to not slip your
   charm into my vulnerable eyes once
   again.

No, we cannot.

We can make this work.

It's tempting
To hear you say you are willing.
To feel that there's hope somewhere in your
    heart.
But making things work takes more than
    words.
It takes letting your heart give life to
    those words,
something I've yet to see from you.

That won't happen.

You've gone silent.

I cannot hear your fingers forming a web
of lies as they cross and overlap different
letters to form those random texts.

There's no perfect messages, no apologies,
no announced empathy lately.

There's no thought bubble forming itself at
the bottom of the iMessage section that
belongs to your name.

Maybe you've given up.

That would make me happy but also sad
that you would give up so quickly.

I miss the attention if I'm being honest.

To feel wanted by the person you once
wanted to cherish your existence comes
with a certain high.

Despite my feelings, I need to let go.

I'll just block and unblock your number as
my emotions find fitting.

You're ignoring me?

Ignoring you has been the best way for my
  heart to find peace.
I'm choosing peace.

crickets

Happy Birthday

Nothing ruins a good birthday like an ex
  showing up unexpectedly in your inbox.
You are taking the happiness out of my
  birthday.
I want this day to be about me,
I want it to be about the life I am currently
  living, which doesn't have a hint of you
  in it.
I want to bring nothing from my past
  into it,
nor do I want to deal with complicated
  feelings today.
Way to wait on this moment to sneak
  yourself back into my memory.
Thank you for waking up the thoughts that
  were resting in the back of my mind.

Thank you.

How did you celebrate your birthday?

Without you.
Without a meaningless dinner in the
    presence of pretentious love.
I spent it with family & friends.
With love in our midst and in a happiness-
    filled air.
I celebrated my birthday free of arguments
    and inauthentic routines.
I truly celebrated, something I haven't
    done in a long time.

Enjoying life without you.

**It's been good knowing you. I'm moving on.
Wish you the best.**

This is not my first break up,
I know how the emotional wave goes and
    how mind games are played.
You want me when I am responsive, but
    when the responses aren't in your favor,
    your blood boils.
You use reverse psychology to get answers
    you deem good signs, but then when it
    turns, you feel like you are being played.
This is not a game. I am not playing hard to
    get. I am not making you work for it.
I will no longer be easy to get.
If there's any chance of this working out,
    you will break many sweats.
You will have to earn my trust, heart,
    and love.

You threatening to leave me alone will
    make me wonder sometimes, but trust
    me, you are threatening me with a
    good time.
Please leave.

K

**Why are you always responding
  with "K"?**

If you believe that "okay" is me
  torturing you,
you are sadly mistaken.
It's how I communicate with people who
  don't deserve words from me.
It's how I acknowledge the past.
K is more than a mouthful when it comes
  to speaking to you.
Maybe it would be better to let silence
  create some guessing games in your mind
  the way you forced it to toy with mine.
This word that you keep finding heartless
  was all you gave me when I poured my
  heart out to you.

Okay.

I don't want to lose you.

Unfortunately, you made sure you did
   everything to lose me.
I spent far too many days unheard,
   unappreciated, and uncared for.
Though my feelings for you are still finding
   their exit,
this reality will have to be something that
   you face.
Maybe this is your lesson to never take
   good things for granted.

You did lose me.

I'm miserable without you.

Miserable was the moment I spent waiting
   on you to wave the white flag and come
   to me on bended knee to acknowledge
   your wrongs.
On the good days, I carried hope on my
   lips, hoping you would come taste it as
   we kissed.
I left second chances at the doorsteps of my
   heart,
hoping you would stop by and see the hint
   that it's a package I want you to carry.
But nope.
None of that happened.
You opened your heart to new dating
   opportunities while masking any pain
   you felt.
You kept me as far away as the sun and the
   moon while we rotated on and off.

crickets

We had good times together.

Isn't it funny, you remember our
    relationship like a salad bar,
Pick and choose which memory will satisfy
    your hunger.
We had great times together,
We also had plenty bad ones under
    our belt.
So bad that we are here,
you finally doing your best to prove your
    love to me
and I, unimpressed, am proving how much
    I wasted my precious love for you.
We had good times together, but the
    relationship wasn't good.

Whatever.

You look nice.

Are you stalking me?
Now I'm easy on the eyes, but when I was
    with you, compliments couldn't find their
    way to your lips.
Thank you, I guess.
But why didn't you make an effort to
    speak to me when you haven't stopped
    texting me?
That's the point, you are still bluffing, still
    full of promises and no action.

Are you stalking me?

You deleted me on Facebook?

I've been deleted out of your life.
The last thing I need is a reminder that
I did not make sure you were deleted
everywhere else.
There's a level of pettiness in me that
wants you to experience my healing and
growth, and see all that I've become
without you, but it's not worth it.

Yes.

Are you with somebody?

No, I am not with anybody,
I am still wallowing in fear, afraid to dip
    my toes in the dating pool once again
    with sharks like you swimming around.
I don't want to drown in something good
    once again only to find out it was shallow,
    a puddle I mistook for the ocean.
I am with nobody because I don't want to
    meet someone like you again.

How's your new friend?

PIERRE ALEX JEANTY

Do you miss me?

Had you asked me this a little bit earlier,
my answer would've been different.
The nights became lonely after you.
My heart howled at the moon hoping yours
would answer the call,
but winter came and ate up all the hope
that was growing in me.
No, I do not miss you.
I am slowly no longer missing what we
used to be.
You have become less than a memory, a
page in my story that has found a home
in the back of my mind.
There was a time I missed you, but that
time is long gone.

NO.

I go back and read our old texts.

Good for you.
I hope that you spot the unnecessary
   arguments you started.
The passive-aggressive behavior.
The way you mishandled my vulnerability.
The misinterpretation of my truth, etc.
I know you are only looking for the good
   you've offered me, but I hope you see the
   bad and realize why I can't pour more
   into anything between us.

Good for you.

You deserve better.

I strongly believe this; I may have said it
without an ounce of belief, but it's true.
I deserved at least an open door to express
my feelings without them being used
against me.
I deserved at least some attention from
someone I'm sharing my heart with.
I deserved at least the same amount of
what I gave to you.
I deserve something that is more for me
and better for soul.
I deserve better and this doesn't mean that
I believe I deserve more than you.
I deserve someone who is more for me.

I know this now.

Can you please help me?

The beautiful thing about our modern
   world is that you can always call someone
   for an emergency.
Call your parents.
Call your friends.
Call the authorities.
Call your local politician.
There are countless people who will help
   you more than I am willing to help you.

I cannot.

PIERRE ALEX JEANTY

Are you busy?

Yes, I am indeed,
busy pouring dirt inside the hole where
   I buried our relationship.
I'm busy erasing your voice, your residue,
   your memory from thoughts.

Stop bothering me.

VISITING SCARS

The night is different,
instead of being chained to the silence of
    my room
and letting the TV entertain me until sleep
    comes to rescue me,
I am outside,
and by outside,
I mean in public places unfazed by the idea
    of running into you.
And, of course, God has its way of putting
    me in situations to prove my strength.
Here you are, somehow existing in the
    same space.
Present in my presence. Face to face.
"Oh hey, how have you been?" your lips
    echoed with awkwardness slipping
    through.
"I've been good. And yourself?"
    I responded, unbothered.
"I've been good," you replied with
    uncertainty in your eyes.

"It was nice seeing you," I replied, hinting
    that this is all the conversation you will
    pull out of me.
You weren't supposed to be here.
I wasn't supposed to be visiting the scars.
However, I am glad to see there's almost no
    pulse between us.

Hey Stranger,
silence
How have you been?
more silence
Can I ask you something?
What is it?
👀
What?
It was nice seeing you again.
Read 11:00 a.m.
I'll never stop fighting for you.
Good for you.
I miss you.
I would miss me, too.
Please don't replace me.
You're replaceable.
good morning 😁
It's 6 a.m.
Come get your stuff back.
Now you want to give them back?
I'm dating now.
more silence

What if I leave them for you?
I'm blocking you.
I'm happy for you.
even more silence
You broke my heart.
What the heck? How??
I hope you are doing well.
Couldn't be better.
I was so good to you.
silence
Why won't you respond to me?
even more silence than before
I've changed.
I guess that's good for you.
Can I call you?
Why do you keep texting me?
I regret losing you.
You'll get over it.
You can trust me again.
No, thanks.
I was a fool.
silence

Good night.

U still love me
Absolutely not.
Happy Thanksgiving

Are you getting my texts?

You gave up on me.
No, you gave up on us.
You didn't deserve that.
I sure didn't.
No one else will want you.
This is why you're an ex.
I'm happy for you.
Thank you, I guess.
**I hope you find someone who will treat
 you better.**
I will.
Without me you are nothing!
Indecisive much?

PIERRE ALEX JEANTY

I just needed some space.
Goodbye.
We once had a great connection.
I still care.
I don't care.
I tried to save us.
Should've done much more than that.
I'm done crying over you.

I wish I never met you.
ignore and dodge guilt trip
Why are you so heartless?
Because of you.
What if we were meant to be?
Well, we weren't.
I've moved on.
Just stop texting me.
Happy New Year's
blocked

Hey Stranger,

Isn't it funny, how this really defines what
   we've become.
Twice strangers.
Once beyond our control, while now it's
   our choices and decisions creating a
   bridge whose purpose is to keep opening
   the distance between our hearts.
Here we are now, the perfect example of
   broken promises.

silence

How have you been?

I'm finally reaching a phase where your
    name holds no weight anymore.
My heart no longer beats for you.
Your attempt to reclaim your place in my
    life doesn't trigger me anymore.
I've been great since I've convinced my
    heart into burying our memory.
I am doing well, well without you.
Thanks for checking in.

more silence

Can I ask you something?

Sure, as long you promise me that you're
   not trying to resurrect us.
Promise me you will not ruin my attempt to
   be amicable.
Promise me that you will not perform
   another act of manipulation and call it an
   attempt to win me back.
Promise me that you will not make me
   regret opening the door a little wider
   when I know it's supposed to be closed.

What is it?

👀

If you're trying to get a pulse on us,
there is none, there's an overextended
    funeral celebration of what we were.
I hope you get the fact that I only respond
    to certain texts
because I am seeing you through platonic
    lenses.

What?

It was nice seeing you again.

It was most definitely nice seeing you.
It was nice seeing how your presence no
    longer chokes air out of me.
My anxiety didn't come running and
    tag-teaming with my awkwardness as
    I expected.
Being unmoved by our eyes meeting each
    other for the first time since it all ended
    was nice.
It was nice seeing my growth.

read 11:00 a.m.

I'll never stop fighting for you.

The way you fight with commitment will
    never convince me otherwise.
But even if you did,
I have no space in my world for your
    existence.
You are now the ashes of the past.
A wound that is now a scar.

Good for you.

I miss you.

Of course, you do.
Everyone misses a good thing.
I gave you everything good that I had and
    an opportunity to be loved genuinely.
You know what you lost and an
    opportunity to take me for granted once
    more will never happen again.
I would miss me, too.
The truth is that sometimes in life, what
    you miss never comes back.
I'm not coming back despite how much
    you miss me.

I would miss me, too.

Please don't replace me.

You're not being replaced.
The position you've held in my life will
    always be vacant.
I promise my heart that I will never auction
    it to someone like you.
I will never settle for being someone's
    afterthought.

You're replaceable.

good morning 😁

There's no way to wake up my desires for
    you before the sun.
There are no desires for you left within me.
Morning texts don't win over people
    you've hurt.
You used this up during the honeymoon
    phase.
Try again in the next life.

It's 6 a.m.

Come get your stuff back.

Like what?
Like the souvenirs that will keep your
   name in my mouth
or the smell of our old things that will keep
   our past breathing.
I don't want any of this back,
I just want all my heart back,
all that I've poured into us back.
I just want my smiles back and my joy
   before you.

Now you want to give them back?

I'm dating now.

Congratulations on making sure I never
  come back to you.
Thank you for making sure any little bit of
  fire between us is put out.
I'm happy that you will be draining
  someone else.
I feel for the next person, this attempt
  to make your ex jealous when you've
  happily moved on is everything that's
  wrong with having a relationship
  with you.
I hope your new person discovers this
  sooner than later.

more silence

What if I leave them for you?

That would make you twice as bad.
The act of choosing me again over the
person you chose over me is all the proof
   I need that you are still the same.
I don't want to be second to anyone.
Neither do I want to be first.
Out of the ocean of humans out there,
   I know there's a fish for me.
I am committed to waiting on the person
   that picks me as the only one.

I'm blocking you.

I'm happy for you.

You should be.
To celebrate someone moving forward
   with bruised knees, scarred legs, and
   determination, dancing to their own
   thumping heart
ought to make anyone cheer them on.
You should be happy for me,
that I am saying goodbye to things in
   my life.
YOU.

even more silence

You broke my heart.

This is not how this works.
You don't get to hurt someone and cry
  about being hurt
because of how they choose to handle
  the hurt.
My choices no longer involve you; you've
  made sure of that.
You broke your own heart, shouting blood
  with the knife in hand.
A classic trick of narcissism. What a
  shame.

What the heck? How??

I hope you are doing well.

I honestly am.
It has been so possible without your
existence in my life.
I have been searching for more than love.
I have put down the weight of my
insecurities.
I have allowed better to find me.
Life is no longer looking at a mirror fogged
up with regret.
Choosing love over myself is now a foolish
idea that I will not fall victim to.
I am doing well carving new paths
without you.
I am doing better knowing that we
are done.

Couldn't be better.

I was so good to you.

Gaslighting much?
How do you counter my reality with your
    perfectly crafted imaginations?
How do you stay married to your truth
    when it is far from the truth itself?
Why do you try so much to remind me of
    the good
    when I have trouble finding it?
You are once again turning this back to
    you when it's not about you.

silence

Why won't you respond to me?

Because I've already given you enough of
   my voice and look where we are.
My silence is everything you deserve and
   much more than I can give you.

even more silence than before

I've changed.

Good for you.
I, too, have changed.
I am no longer waiting on your apology;
I apologized enough to myself for
   surrendering to your mess.

I guess that's good for you.

Can I call you?

For what?
To try your foolish magic trick where you
  pull the most loving words out of your
  hat of lies and tell me words that promise
  a better you in my future?
To keep me from the better me who doesn't
  need you in my future?
You cannot call me.
You shouldn't even be texting me,
but I still need a reminder for my broken
  heart to know what types of strangers to
  stay away from.

Why do you keep texting me?

I regret losing you.

The thing with regret is that sometimes
we realize how the bed we made for
ourselves feels when we cuddle up with
the consequences and hug tightly the
results.
It's the raunchy smell of our decisions
when we realize the outcome is
completely different.
Of course, you regret losing me,
just as I spent time regretting everything
that led to our story.
But I've learned that it was just part of
my journey.
This is part of your journey.

You'll get over it.

You can trust me again.

Trust is not a yo-yo,
You don't drop it as you please and
    summon it back as you'd like.
You killed my trust for you and expect it to
    resurrect just because you're tired of it no
    longer existing for you.
I do not trust those who mix love with
    consistent actions that look nothing
    like love.

No, thanks.

I was a fool.

Yes, you were.
I was even more of a fool for not believing
   my eyes when they pointed at the truth.

silence

PIERRE ALEX JEANTY

Good night.

The nights are truly good now.
When light starts to crack into the dark sky,
the sun is no longer greeting me with
    wet eyes
or eyes with bags full of the sadness from
    yesterday's mess.
The nights are great now.
I leave yesterday's moments behind and
    prepare myself for tomorrow.
A tomorrow without you,
a tomorrow that is better than it was
    before you.
A tomorrow where you don't belong to me,
    but my heart finally does.

U still love me

And you still love you, too.
Still in love with lack of commitment.
Still engaged to your ego.
Still married to your old ways.
Find someone else to stroke your ego.

Absolutely not.

PIERRE ALEX JEANTY

Happy Thanksgiving

Using the holiday to pop back up out of
   nowhere.
Like a game of whack-a-mole, I will hit
   every attempt on the head.
Reaching out during the time my family
   will question your absence is slick,
but I've been bitten enough to know you're
   still a snake.

Are you getting my texts?

Yes, I hope you got the clue.
Please understand my silence will be
   your reward.

You gave up on me.

I did not give up on you.
I did not give up on the relationship.
I gave up on the idea of trying to fix
   something that is broken when the other
   person keeps doing more breaking.
I gave up on idea of unconditional loyalty,
   and I will not try to create joy where it
   has found a way in.
I never gave up on you until you gave up
   on us.

No, you gave up on us.

You didn't deserve that.

But it's what I got, it's what you served me
    on a cold platter.
A heart fighting for its breath while it looks
    for strength to gather itself together.
You're right, I never deserved that, it's
    unfortunate that I've come to realize
    that after I realized that you didn't
    deserve me.
I guess it's safe to say we both got what we
    didn't deserve.

I sure didn't.

No one else will want you.

But you do, your lips are looking for ways
to say my name sweeter.
You and people like you want me. I have
all these texts to prove it.
It's unfortunate that you've come to this,
but I understand the obsession with
wanting what you can't have.

This is why you're an ex.

I'm happy for you.

Why do you insist on interrupting my
   happiness?
I don't mean to sound rude, but you no
   longer being in my life has left the door
   open for happiness to find its way in.
I am glad that you are seeing happiness on
   me, but let's not forget that along the way
   you became the reason happiness kept
   itself away from me.
I am glad that you are seeing what you
   took from me.

Thank you, I guess.

PIERRE ALEX JEANTY

**I hope you find someone who will treat
  you better.**

I hope so, too.
I've met enough people looking for less
  than forever that I cannot wait to meet
  one who is at least here to meet death
  with me.
It's exhausting to keep trying to see if they
  are right and check off another list of
  people you got it wrong with.

I will.

Without me you are nothing!

Here it is, your anger proving to me that
  I've made the right choice to stay as far
  as the seas from you.
I am nothing if I am not yours, yet you
  treated me as nothing when I was yours.
I am nothing to you.
Knowing this gave me everything I needed
  to keep this chapter closed.
To be everything I need to be is all I desire
  now. Being nothing to you is just enough
  to keep me away.
And please stop letting your anger turn
  nothing into something about you.
I want nothing to do with you. It's that
  simple.

Indecisive much?

I just needed some space.

Here you are with all the space in the
    world, still trying to get me to reclaim the
    space I once occupied in your life.

Goodbye.

We once had a great connection.

This is true, but you disconnected it.
You failed at every act of service there is
    while lowering the bar.
We couldn't stay synchronized.
We saw "us" through different lenses.

I still care.

Care for what?
Why did you convince me that you didn't
    with your actions?
Why did you send your absence to tell me
    that you don't?
Why didn't you show me that you cared
    when I begged for it?
Why am I even entertaining conversations
    with you?
This is what you want.
To get a rise out of me, to get me to spill all
    my thoughts and create a conversation.
You will not find an emotional trigger.
No entry.
Bye.

I don't care.

I tried to save us.

Putting effort toward the wrong things
   isn't supposed to give us the outcome
   we desire.
Good intentions give birth to many more
   bad endings than we realize.
We didn't need to be saved.
We needed to be maintained.

Should've done much more than that.

PIERRE ALEX JEANTY

I'm done crying over you.

What a pleasant surprise, that you shed
    tears thinking of me.
That my name has found a way to crack
    through your emotions.
What an honor it is to be the one to cause
    the tears to fall.

I wish I never met you.

Confusion will hold you by the throat and
  slowly extract every drip of happiness
  out of you.
Trying to float on a wave of emotion with
  nothing but faded memories will do that
  to you.
On some days, the memories will keep a
  smile on your face, and on other days, it
  will only offer you sadness.
I know where you are at, an island of
  misplaced anger trying to swim toward
  something you want that doesn't seem to
  want you.
I was there when my wounds were fresh,
  and my heart wanted your hands to do
  the fixing.
I found it.

ignore and dodge guilt trip

Why are you so heartless?

I will not pack my emotions and join you
  on this guilt trip.
I will not get sucked into your
  victimization.
You've given me more than enough reasons
  to be heartless, but I still resisted.
I resisted the opportunity to be numb, cold,
  and ugly.
This is not being heartless; this is the fruit
  of someone who isn't letting their heart
  think more of you than you are.

Because of you.

What if we were meant to be?

When did you realize this?
When you begged me to pour all of me into
   your hands?
Is that when you realized your hands were
   not ready to hold the responsibility of
   cherishing someone's heart?
Was it when you carried conversations
   about the future you've always been
   afraid of?
When did you realize you weren't ready for
   all that we could've been?
Was it when you couldn't stop taking?

Well, we weren't.

I've moved on.

Good for you, though you announcing it to
 me is proof that you've yet to change.
Always moving forward while dragging
 your past with you.
Always trying to see where an ex can be
 fit in.
I hope the person who gives you a chance
 to love them doesn't suffer you the way
 I had to.

Just stop texting me.

Happy New Year's

It's finally time to leave you behind.

blocked

There's no notification fighting for space on
my screen with your name on it anymore.
My imagination isn't creating scenarios of
what you might possibly be doing, saying
about me, doing with someone else.
My heart feels empty of you and full of me.
The mourning is finally over.
Our story is now just ashes being scattered
by the wind.
I will acknowledge your existence,
but as far as your presence in my life, it's
almost forgotten.
The lessons will never leave, but as for you,
you are gone.
I've grown too kind and dedicated to my
heart to ever grow bitter, petty, or numb.
So wanting nothing to do with you has
nothing to do with the hurt, with what
happened with us.

I'm not turning a new page into a new
   chapter.
I'm starting a different book, embracing a
   new story.
I am finally here. At the other side of this.
Goodbye.

Andrews McMeel Publishing
a division of Andrews McMeel Universal
1130 Walnut Street, Kansas City, Missouri 64106

www.andrewsmcmeel.com

24 25 26 27 28 KPR 10 9 8 7 6 5 4 3 2 1

ISBN: 978-1-5248-8065-1

Library of Congress Control Number: 2023948110

Editor: Patty Rice
Art Director/Designer: Julie Barnes
Production Editor: Jennifer Straub
Production Manager: Shona Burns

ATTENTION: SCHOOLS AND BUSINESSES

Andrews McMeel books are available at quantity discounts with bulk purchase for educational, business, or sales promotional use. For information, please e-mail the Andrews McMeel Publishing Special Sales Department: sales@amuniversal.com.